MW01484242

# Supervision for Civil Service Exams

Lewis Morris

Copyright © 2019, Network4Learning, Inc.

All rights reserved.

ISBN: 1530419948
ISBN-13: 978-1530419944

# DEDICATION

This work is dedicated to all my students whose enthusiasm and hard work made this book possible.

If you found this book helpful, please consider writing a review at:
http://www.amazon.com/review/create-review?&asin=1530419948

For more resources visit:
https://insiderswords.com/supervision-for-civil-service-exams/

# CONTENTS

Acknowledgments i

1 About Supervision Questions on Civil Service Exams 3

2 Supervisory Best Practices 5

3 Sexual Harassment 9

4 Interview Questions 12

5 Laws and agencies Affecting Employment and Supervision 14

6 Supervision Competencies 17

7 Supervision Question Sample Set 19

8 Supervision Questions and Answers 26

8 Answers to Practice Questions 66

10 Glossary 84

# ACKNOWLEDGMENT

The publishers would like to acknowledge the hard work and talent of Gabrielle Morris who did the layout and graphic design of this work.

# About Supervision Questions on Civil Service Exams

Many civil service exams that test for upper-level positions require the candidate to complete a battery of questions that test supervision and administrative skills and competencies. The questions will be based on scenarios where a candidate must decide on the best course of action or based on management theories and laws.

For the supervision sub-area, there are three types of supervision skills tested:

Supervision: These questions test for knowledge of the principles and practices employed in planning, organizing, and controlling the activities of a work unit toward predetermined objectives. The concepts covered, usually in a situational question format, include such topics as assigning and reviewing work; evaluating performance; maintaining work standards; motivating and developing subordinates; implementing procedural change; increasing efficiency; and dealing with problems of absenteeism, morale, and discipline.

Administrative Supervision: These questions test for knowledge of the principles and practices involved in directing the activities of a large subordinate staff, including subordinate supervisors. Questions relate to the personal interactions between an upper-level supervisor and his/her subordinate supervisors in the accomplishment of objectives. These questions cover such areas as assigning work to and coordinating the activities of several units, establishing and guiding staff development programs, evaluating the performance of subordinate supervisors, and maintaining relationships with other organizational sections.

Supervision Theories and Laws: These questions are straight academic questions that assess the candidate's knowledge of key management theories, landmark laws, and vocabulary.

3

# Guidelines for Supervisory candidates

1. **Establish objective** levels of work performance. For example, All Clerks are responsible for clearing their assigned list before the close of business every day.

2. **Measure, Evaluate and Record** job performance. Specific, behavioral criteria are necessary. For example, all employees will complete seven packets per hour with an accuracy of 97%.

3. **Be Honest** and speak with authority. **Example:** "You are a valued employee, but I expect you to complete your assigned tasks every day."

4. **Focus on performance, not personality. Be Specific:** "I observed that you left your work unfinished at the end of today's shift."

5. **Be Consistent** in your expectations of employees. For example, all employees at this pay grade must complete the task each shift.

6. **Prompt reprimand for all disciplinary matters.** You want to stop unwanted behavior and be able to discuss the incident when it is fresh in an employee's mind.

7. **Get a Commitment from the employee to improve specific behaviors: Example:** "Here is a list of tasks you must complete each shift, I will give you a copy, and I will keep one. Do we have an agreement?"

8. **Follow-up**: Meet with the employee after a specific amount of time. **Supervisor**: "We will meet next Tuesday at 2:00 PM to review the changes we have agreed to."

# Supervisory Best Practices

A Supervisor's goal is to establish a work environment that is healthy and productive for all employees. It is important for supervisors to focus on objective performance standards when evaluating an employee's job performance.

Supervisors may have to intervene when employees are having difficulty. Employees who are having difficulty often exhibit the following:
1. Frequent absences with vague excuses.
2. Excessive use of sick days
3. Pattern of unscheduled time off.
4. Repeatedly coming to work late.
5. Repeated early departures from work.
6. Taking days off following a weekend, holiday or vacation.
7. Using up vacation days as soon as they are accrued.
8. Frequent unannounced absences during assigned work hours.
9. Repeatedly missing scheduled staff meetings or client-related activities.
10. Errors in judgment, which are inconsistent with past standards of good judgment.
11. Difficulty or failure to carry out routine instructions.
12. Erratic or deteriorating quality of performance when compared with past performance.
13. Overreacting to appropriate criticism.
14. Manipulating co-workers to take over assigned responsibilities.
15. Avoiding interaction with co-workers.
16. Appearing withdrawn or overly preoccupied.
17. Wide mood swings during the day for no apparent reason.
18. An increase in personal telephone calls causing repeated work interruptions.
19. Deteriorating hygiene or appearance.
20. Complaints by co-workers about employee's erratic behavior or lack of work cooperation.

The supervisor should write down specific information regarding performance problems. Complete and accurate documentation will enable a supervisor to:
1.   Be objective, fair and consistent.
2.   Present factual and objective information that gives the employee a clear picture of their job performance.
3.   Prepare a written plan for corrective action.
4.   Documentation is necessary if disciplinary action is taken.

Supervisors should address only job-performance problems. Meeting with employees to discuss performance problems should be private. The supervisor should describe job performance problems in behavioral terms. Before meeting with your employee, discuss your observations and get support from your supervisor. Meet and discuss with your immediate supervisor, the data collected and formulate a plan to approach the employee.

**When it becomes necessary to have a disciplinary meeting with an employee:**
1.   Inform the employee of the purpose of the meeting.
2.   Give the employee a copy of your documentation.
3.   Be fair, firm and clear about what the employee is expected to do to improve their job performance.
4.   Be a patient listener. Allow the employee an opportunity to explain their actions and what problems they are experiencing.
5.   Get a commitment from the employee that they understand and accept the plan for improvement. Give them a copy of the plan.
6.   Keep confidential any information the employee tells you about their personal problems.
7.   Be consistent with workplace rules and regulations.
8.   Set a reasonable date for a follow-up meeting to review the employee's progress.
9.   Inform the employee that they have the ultimate responsibility for the improvement of job performance.

## What not to do
1. Don't try to diagnose a personal/drug or alcohol problem.
2. Do not preach, lecture or "brow beat" an employee
3. Do not attempt to manipulate the employee.
4. Don't judge or moralize.
5. Don't threaten disciplinary action, unless there will be follow through.
6. Don't engage in rumors, deal only in facts.
7. Don't be diverted from the purpose of the meeting by arguing.
8. Don't accept excuses or alibis.
9. Don't talk about the activities of other employees.
10. Don't set unreasonable goals for improvement. It took time for the problem to develop, and it will take time to correct.

## Follow Through
Schedule a follow-up meeting within 2-4 weeks after the initial performance evaluation. During the interim, continue to observe and document job performance. Follow up meetings with employees are important because they enable both parties to assess improvement or lack of improvement. The outcome of a second meeting may be that no further meetings are needed or that subsequent ones would be helpful.

## Supervisor Do's
Continuously monitor the employee's job performance.

Document specific actions and behavior.

Remediate as close to the occurrence as possible.

Counsel the employee in a private place.

Present specific, objective information on job performance from your documentation.

Set up a plan to improve performance.

Ask the employee if he/she understands the situation clearly. If necessary, restate and check for understanding.

Set a specific time and date to review the situation.

## Supervisor Don'ts

Don't generalize about the employee's job performance or use subjective terms.

Don't criticize outside behavior. Restrict your evaluation to job performance.

Don't cover up for an employee that is failing. Misguided kindness can lead to a serious delay in the employee receiving help.

Don't cut-off an employee. Hear them out.

Don't bargain with employees

Never threaten an employee.

Don't ask employees to do anything unethical.

Don't spy on your employees.

Don't create a policy every time somebody messes up.

# Sexual Harassment

Some supervision questions address the topic of sexual harassment.

Sexual Harassment Sexual harassment is a form of sex discrimination that violates Title VII of the Civil Rights Act of 1964. Title VII applies to employers with 15 or more employees, including state and local governments. It applies to employment agencies and labor organizations, as well as to the federal government. Unwelcome sexual advances, requests for sexual favors, and other verbal or physical conduct of a sexual nature constitute sexual harassment when this conduct explicitly or implicitly affects an individual's employment, unreasonably interferes with an individual's work performance, or creates an intimidating, hostile, or offensive work environment. Sexual harassment can occur in a variety of circumstances, including but not limited to the following:

The victim, as well as the harasser, may be a woman or a man.

The victim does not have to be of the opposite sex.

The harasser can be the victim's supervisor, an agent of the employer, a supervisor in another area, a co-worker, or a non-employee.

The victim does not have to be the person harassed but could be anyone affected by the offensive conduct.

Unlawful sexual harassment may occur without economic injury to or discharge of the victim.

The harasser's conduct must be unwelcome. It is helpful for the victim to inform the harasser directly that the conduct is unwelcome and must stop.

The victim should use any employer complaint mechanism or grievance system available. When investigating allegations of sexual harassment, the Equal Employment Opportunity Commission looks at the whole record: the circumstances, such as the nature of the sexual advances, and the context in which the alleged incidents occurred. A determination on the allegations is made from the facts on a case-by-case basis. Prevention is the best tool to eliminate sexual harassment in the workplace. Employers are encouraged to take steps necessary to prevent sexual harassment from occurring. They should clearly communicate to employees that sexual harassment will not be tolerated. They can do so by providing sexual harassment training to their employees and by establishing an effective complaint or grievance process and taking immediate and appropriate action when an employee complains. It is also unlawful to retaliate against an individual for opposing employment practices that discriminate based on sex or for filing a discrimination charge, testifying, or participating in any way in an investigation, proceeding, or litigation under Title VII.

Below is a sample sexual harassment policy that spells out what sexual harassment is and how it should be dealt with.

SAMPLE SEXUAL HARASSMENT POLICY

It is the policy of (Agency Name) that all employees are responsible for ensuring that the workplace is free from sexual harassment. Because of (Agency's Name) strong disapproval of offensive or inappropriate sexual behavior at work, all employees must avoid any action or conduct which could be viewed as sexual harassment. Sexual harassment includes unwelcome sexual advances, requests for sexual favors, and other verbal or physical conduct of a sexually harassing nature, when:

(1) Submission to the harassment is made either explicitly or implicitly a term or condition of employment;

(2) Submission to or rejection of the harassment is used as the basis for employment decisions affecting the individual; or

(3) The harassment has the purpose or effect of unreasonably interfering with an individual's work performance or creating an intimidating, hostile, or offensive working environment.

Any employee who has a complaint of sexual harassment at work by anyone, including supervisors, co-workers or visitors, should first clearly inform the harasser that his/her behavior is offensive or unwelcome and request that the behavior stop. If the behavior continues, the employee must immediately bring the matter to the attention of his/her supervisor. If the immediate supervisor is involved in the harassing activity, the violation should be reported to that supervisor's immediate supervisor, the department personnel officer, or the employee relations coordinator, who can be reached at (phone number). If a supervisor or personnel officer knows of an incident of sexual harassment, they shall take appropriate remedial action immediately. If the alleged harassment involves any types of threats of physical harm to the victim, the alleged harasser may be suspended with pay. During such suspension, an investigation will be conducted by (Agency Name). If the investigation supports charges of sexual harassment, disciplinary action against the alleged harasser will take place and may include termination. If the investigation reveals that the charges were brought falsely, the charging party may be subject to disciplinary action.

When dealing with sexual harassment, it is wise to refer to a stated policy for the agency. If that is not available, then the next course of action would be to take any complaint seriously, move the complaint up the chain of command, and document the complaint as carefully as possible. Never try to bargain a solution between the offender and victim, and never try to handle the situation alone.

# Interview Questions

Some Supervision questions focus on the interview process. Often there is some confusion as to what appropriate, legal questions are. Below is a sample of illegal questions and some options for correcting them.

Ask only job-related questions.

It is illegal not to hire candidates because of their race, color, sex, religion, national origin, birthplace, age, disability or marital/family status. Do not ask questions that could elicit such information, and discourage candidates from volunteering personal details. Illegal/inappropriate questions:

Questions related to birthplace, ancestry or national origin: … "How long has your family been in the U.S.?" … "That's an unusual name—what does it mean?" … "How did you learn to speak Chinese?"

Acceptable question: "Are you eligible to work in the U.S.?"

Questions related to marital status, children or pregnancy: "Are you planning to have children?", "What does your husband/wife do?", "What are your child care arrangements?"

Acceptable question: "Would you be able to work a 9:00 a.m. to 6:00 p.m. schedule?"(If asked of all applicants and a specific work schedule is a business necessity)

Questions related to physical disability, health or medical history: "Are you able to use your legs at all?", "Do you have any pre-existing health conditions?", "Are you on any medication?" „

Acceptable question: "Can you perform the essential functions of the job, with or without reasonable accommodation?"

Questions related to religion or religious days observed: "What is your religious affiliation?", "What religious holidays do you celebrate?", "Do you attend church every week?"

Acceptable question: "Can you work on weekends?" (If asked of all applicants and weekend work is a business necessity)

Questions related to age: "How old are you?", "What year were you born?", "I went to high school in Oakland, too—what year did you graduate?"

Acceptable question: "Are you over the age of 18?"

Questions related to criminal records: "Have you ever been arrested?", "Have you ever spent a night in jail?", "Have you ever been caught driving drunk?"

Acceptable question: "Have you ever been convicted of a crime?"

Other illegal questions: "Was your military discharge honorable or dishonorable?", "Have you ever brought a lawsuit against an employer?", "Have you ever filed for Workers' Compensation?", "Have you ever been sexually harassed?", "How much do you weigh?", "Do you use drugs or alcohol?"

# Laws and agencies Affecting Employment and Supervision

**The Americans with Disabilities Act of** 1990 (ADA) is a law that was enacted by the U.S. Congress in 1990. In 1986, the National Council on Disability had recommended the enactment of an Americans with Disabilities Act (ADA) and drafted the first version of the bill which was introduced in the House and Senate in 1988. The ADA was signed into law on July 26, 1990, by President George H. W. Bush, amended and signed by President George W. Bush with changes effective January 1, 2009.

The ADA is a wide-ranging civil rights law that is intended to protect against discrimination based on disability. It affords similar protections against discrimination to Americans with disabilities as the Civil Rights Act of 1964, which made discrimination based on race, religion, sex, national origin, and other characteristics illegal. Unlike the Civil Rights Act, the ADA also requires covered employers to provide reasonable accommodations to employees with disabilities and imposes accessibility requirements on public accommodations.
The Americans With Disabilities Act, known as ADA, was signed into law on July 26, 1990. It carried forward material from Section 504 of the Rehabilitation Act of 1973. A 'reasonable accommodation' is defined by the US Department of Justice as "any modification or adjustment to a job or the work environment that will enable a qualified applicant or employee with a disability to participate in the application process or to perform essential job functions. Reasonable accommodation also includes adjustments to assure that a qualified individual with a disability has rights and privileges in employment equal to those of employees without disabilities."

**Section 504 of the Rehabilitation Act of 1973**, Pub. L. No. 93-112, 87 Stat. 394 (Sept. 26, 1973), codified at 29 U.S.C. § 701 et seq., is American legislation that guarantees certain rights to people with disabilities. It was the first U.S. federal civil rights protection for people with disabilities. Because it was successfully implemented over the next several years, it helped to pave the way for the Virginians with Disabilities Act in 1985 and the 1990 Americans with Disabilities Act.

Section 504 states (in part): No otherwise qualified individual with a disability in the United States, as defined in section 705(20) of this title, shall, solely by reason of her or his disability, be excluded from the participation in, be denied the benefits of, or be subjected to discrimination under any program or activity receiving Federal financial assistance or under any program or activity conducted by any Executive agency or by the United States Postal Service.

As amended in 1974,Section 111, Pub L. 93-516, 88 Stat. 1619 (Dec. 7, 1974), Individuals with Disabilities are: any person who (A) has a physical or mental impairment which substantially limits one or more of such person's major life activities, (B) has a record of such an impairment, or (C) is regarded as having such an impairment where "Major life activities include caring for one's self, walking, seeing, hearing, speaking, breathing, working, performing manual tasks, and learning."

**However, "For purposes of employment", Qualified Individuals with Disabilities must also meet "normal and essential eligibility requirements", such that: "For purposes of employment, Qualified Individuals with Disabilities are persons who, with Reasonable Accommodation, can perform the essential functions of the job for which they have applied or have been hired to perform. "**

**The Civil Rights Act of 1964** is a landmark piece of civil rights legislation in the United States that outlawed discrimination based on race, color, religion, sex, or national origin. It ended unequal application of voter registration requirements and racial segregation in schools, at the workplace and by facilities that served the general public (known as "public accommodations").

**The Occupational Safety and Health Administration (OSHA)** is an agency of the United States Department of Labor. Congress established the agency under the Occupational Safety and Health Act, which President Richard M. Nixon signed into law on December 29, 1970. OSHA's mission is to "assure safe and healthful working conditions for working men and women by setting and enforcing standards and by providing training, outreach, education and assistance." The agency is also charged with enforcing a variety of whistleblower statutes and regulations.

## Equal Employment Opportunity Commission

The U.S. Equal Employment Opportunity Commission (EEOC) is responsible for enforcing federal laws that make it illegal to discriminate against a job applicant or an employee because of the person's race, color, religion, sex (including pregnancy), national origin, age (40 or older), disability or genetic information. It is also illegal to discriminate against a person because the person complained about discrimination, filed a charge of discrimination, or participated in an employment discrimination investigation or lawsuit.

Most employers with at least 15 employees are covered by EEOC laws (20 employees in age discrimination cases). Most labor unions and employment agencies are also covered.

The laws apply to all types of work situations, including hiring, firing, promotions, harassment, training, wages, and benefits.

# Supervision Competencies

The supervision sub-area questions test various competencies that have been established as necessary for effective supervision. The list below defines those competencies to help you understand what is being tested.

PROBLEM-SOLVING – Identifies and analyzes problems; uses sound reasoning to arrive at conclusions; finds alternative solutions to complex problems; distinguishes between relevant and irrelevant information to make logical judgments.

LEADERSHIP – Leaders inspire, motivate, guide and direct others toward goal accomplishment. Leaders coach, support, mentor, and challenge subordinates; they adapt leadership styles to a variety of situations. Effective leaders will inspire others by modeling high standards of behavior (e.g. courage, honesty, trust, openness, and respect for others, etc.) and by applying these values to daily behaviors.

DECISION-MAKING – Makes sound and well-informed decisions; perceives the impact and implications of decisions; commits to action and causes change, even in uncertain situations, to accomplish organizational goals.

INTERPERSONAL SKILL – Considers and responds appropriately to the needs, feelings, and capabilities of others; adjusts approaches to suit different people and situations. Develops and maintains collaborative and effective working relationships with others.

HUMAN RESOURCE MANAGEMENT – Empowers people by sharing power and authority; develops lower levels of leadership by pushing authority downward and outward throughout the organization; shares rewards for achievement with employees; ensures that staff are appropriately selected, utilized, appraised, and developed and that they are treated in a fair and equitable manner.

COMMUNICATION – Expresses facts and ideas both orally and in writing in a succinct, clear, accurate, thorough, organized and effective manner. Reviews, proofreads and edits written work constructively. Presents facts to individuals or groups effectively; makes clear convincing oral presentations; listens to others; facilitates an open exchange of ideas.

TEAM BUILDING – Manages group processes; encourages and facilitates cooperation, pride, trust, and group identity; fosters commitment and team spirit; works with others to achieve goals.

CONFLICT MANAGEMENT – Manages and resolves conflicts, confrontations, and disagreements in a positive and constructive manner to minimize negative personal impact.

MANAGEMENT - Manages and resolves conflicts, confrontations, and disagreements in a positive and constructive manner to minimize negative personal impact.

PROCESS IMPROVEMENT - Develops new insights into situations and associated processes. Applies innovative solutions to make organizational improvements; designs and implements new or cutting-edge programs/processes.

# Supervision Sample Question Set

Read through one question at a time and attempt to answer it. Immediately review the solution dialogue to give you a better understanding of how and why the correct answer was selected.

Task: You will be presented with situations in which you must apply knowledge of the principles and practices of administrative supervision to answer the questions correctly. You will be placed in the role of a supervisor of a section, which is made up of several units. Each unit has a supervisor and several employees. All unit supervisors report directly to you.

Sample Question 1: In a hallway, you observe two employees strongly arguing about which one of them is responsible for a set of tasks in a collaborative work project that you have delegated to two unit supervisors in your section. The arguing employees work for different units. Which one of the following actions is most appropriate for you to take in this situation?

a. Intercede in the employees' argument and settle it.

b. Meet with the unit supervisors of the two employees and inform them of the situation you observed.

c. Inform one unit supervisor of the situation and ask this supervisor to take care of it.

d. Set up a meeting that includes both unit supervisors and both employees to resolve the situation.

Solution: Choice A is not correct. It is not reasonable that you would be able to settle the employees' dispute. Earlier you delegated the work project to two unit supervisors, who would normally be responsible for assigning tasks related to the project.

The two unit supervisors must be consulted. Choice B is the correct answer to this question. The two unit supervisors are collaborating on the work project and therefore giving the assignments. You should meet with them and tell them about the employees' argument and the work tasks they discussed. Along with learning the point of contention, it is useful for the unit supervisors to learn that two employees had a heated argument. The unit supervisors can work out a way to handle the situation. Choice C is not correct. Speaking to only one supervisor about the situation leaves the second supervisor uninformed of the situation. You cannot be assured that the first supervisor will even include the second supervisor in finding a way to settle the issue. In taking this action, you are favoring one supervisor and slighting the other. Choice D is not correct. The unit supervisors need to come up with a way of handling the situation that you observed. To do this, they must be informed without the employees present. Also, by including the employees in the meeting, you may get a replay of the hallway argument, which is not helpful.

Sample Question 2: Assume the unit you supervise is given a new work assignment and that you are unsure about the proper procedure to use in performing this assignment. Which one of the following actions should you take FIRST in this situation?

a. Obtain input from your staff.

b. Consult other unit supervisors who have had similar assignments.

c. Use an appropriate procedure from a similar assignment that you worked on.

d. Discuss the matter with your supervisor.

Solution: This question asks for the action that you should take FIRST in this situation. Choice A is not correct. Since this assignment is new for your unit, your staff would not be expected to be more knowledgeable than you about the proper procedure. Choice B is not correct. Although discussing this matter with other supervisors may increase your knowledge of the new assignment, similar assignments performed in other units may differ in some important way from your new assignment. Other units may also function differently from your unit, so the procedures used to perform similar assignments may differ accordingly. Choice C is not correct. Since this assignment is new for your unit, you would have no way of knowing whether the procedure from a similar assignment is appropriate to use. You would need someone with the appropriate knowledge, usually your supervisor, to determine if the procedure from a similar assignment could be used before you employed this procedure in the performance of your new assignment. Choice D is the correct answer to this question. Your supervisor is more likely to be informed about what procedure may be appropriate for work that he or she assigns to you than would other unit supervisors or your staff. Even if your supervisor does not know what procedure is appropriate, a decision regarding which procedure to use should be made with his or her participation, since he or she has the ultimate responsibility for your unit's work.

Sample Question 3: A new employee is assigned to the unit that you supervise. Which one of the following is most important to consider when you set training objectives for this employee?

a. the educational level of the employee at the time of hire

b. the typical volume of work produced by the senior employee in the unit

c. the current production level of the unit

d. the performance standards established by the workplace

Solution: Choice A is not correct. While the educational level of the employee may affect how the training is given, it is not strongly linked to training objectives. A training objective is typically a standard of job performance that an employee can successfully demonstrate at the completion of training. This standard is stable and does not vary with the educational level of the employee who is receiving training. Choice B is not correct. The senior employee's typical work volume may not necessarily meet the acceptable standard. Also, this choice deals with only the volume of work; your training objectives should also concern quality of work. Choice C is not correct. The current production level of the unit may be higher or lower than the acceptable standard. Also, like choice B, this choice deals only with work quantity, not quality. Choice D is the correct answer to this question. The workplace must set performance standards for all work activities that are critical to the job so that supervisors can determine whether the work is being successfully performed or whether work product goals are being met. You, as supervisor, must use these performance standards as your training objectives and train the new employee to meet the standards.

Sample Question 4: Which one of the following is the most important reason to record a new policy in writing once it has been adopted?

a. to ensure the acceptance of the new policy by staff

b. to minimize confusion in the interpretation of the new policy

c. to stop the practice of giving special consideration to individual cases

d. to ensure that the policy is integrated into the organization's mission

Solution: This question asks for the most important reason to record a new policy in writing. Choice A is not correct. Staff must be brought into the process of policy development before the policy is adopted to decrease possible staff resistance to the new policy. Choice B is the correct answer to this question. The written record of the policy will serve as the definitive reference for issues or situations that the policy covers. Choice C is not correct. Organizational policies serve as a guide to provide consistency in decision-making for those cases that are covered by the policy, but no policy will cover every possible circumstance or situation. There may be exceptional cases with special circumstances that are not fully covered by the policy. These exceptional cases must be considered individually on a case by case basis. Choice D is not correct. Having a policy in writing will not ensure that the policy is integrated into the organization's mission. Integration of the policy into the organization's mission should have occurred when the policy was being drafted. The correct answer to this sample question is B.

Sample Question 5: Assume that you have called a staff meeting of unit supervisors to resolve a complex problem affecting police response to certain types of criminal activities. Which one of the following is the FIRST action that you should take at this meeting?

a. Define the problem for your staff.

b. Present your proposed solution to the problem.

c. Ask staff for their viewpoints on the problem.

d. Form a committee to study the problem.

Solution: This question asks for the action that you should take FIRST in this situation. When considering the choices, you should identify the choice that describes the action you must take before any of the others. Choice A is the correct answer to this question. A problem must be defined before a solution to it can be developed; and if your staff works collaboratively on a solution, they should all have the same understanding of what the problem is. Choice B is not correct. Before staff can evaluate whether your proposed solution is appropriate, they must have a clear understanding of the nature of the problem. Choice C is not correct. It is not possible to obtain staff viewpoints regarding the problem unless they know what the problem is. Choice D is not correct. You have called this staff meeting to resolve a certain problem, so you and your unit supervisors should be the ones who will "study" the problem. If a committee must be formed for some reason, the problem must still be defined before a determination can be made regarding who is best suited to be on the committee.

Sample Question 6: Sergeant Jacobs is part of a special team of officers who are responsible for attending career fairs on college campuses to recruit entry level Sheriff's Officers. As a routine part of his job, Sergeant Jacobs communicates with university administration to determine when these career fairs will be held so that officers can be scheduled to attend. As a result of workload demands, Sergeant Jacobs decides to delegate this task to one of his subordinate officers who is also a member of the recruitment team. Sergeant Jacobs knows that by delegating this routine task to his subordinate, he is

(a) giving his subordinate officer an opportunity to grow professionally.

(b) no longer responsible for the task.

(c) guaranteeing that his subordinate officer will perform this task correctly.

(d) contributing to his own elimination from the organization as a "surplus" staff member.

Solution: The correct answer is choice (a). In delegating this task, the sergeant is still responsible for its completion. The sergeant is also allowing his subordinate officer the chance to grow and develop, while still being supervised. This experience will add to the quality and ability of the team as a whole.

# Supervision Questions and Answers

1. One of your employees applied for special training a few months-ago and has heard nothing. She states that a friend in another unit got a response almost immediately. Which is your best response?

a. Offer to call about it.

b. Offer to submit a letter in support of the application.

c. Tell the employee to call the training office and see if the application was lost.

d. Offer her your condolences at not being accepted into the program.


2. The planning that supervisors do is directly derived from plans of ...

a. customers.

b. subordinates.

c. upper management.

d. colleagues.

3. Which of the following organizations regulates worker safety?

a. Occupational Safety and Health Administration (OSHA)

b. ANSI

c. United States Department of Labor

d. American Federation of Labor


4. Which of the following is an example of a line employee?

a. A consulting engineer.

b. A sales representative.

c. A security guard.

d. An assembly floor foreman.


5. Employee counseling is usually NOT appropriate for addressing an employee's...

a. marital problems.

b. drinking problem.

c. career planning.

d. retirement planning.

6. When a prospective employee is being interviewed, which of the following questions CANNOT be asked?

a. "Do you have any training that qualifies you for this job?"

b. "Are you over 18 years old?"

c. "What is your marital status?"

d. "Are you in this country on a visa that permits you to work?"

7. Which of the following persons developed the theory of a hierarchy of needs?

a. Douglas McGregor

b. Rensis Likert

c. Abraham Maslow

d. Kurt Lewin

8. Maintenance of departmental discipline in a factory is the function of the…

a. senior employees.

b. supervisor.

c. president.

d. shop steward.

9. All of the following are steps in the controlling process EXCEPT...

a. establishing performance standards.

b. developing employee benefits.

c. monitoring performance.

d. taking corrective action.

10. Which of the following organizations has the power to enforce basic labor laws?

a. National Labor Relations Board

b. Federal Mediation and Conciliation Service

c. United States Department of Labor

d. American Federation of Labor

11. Which of the following organizations is a labor union?

a. National Labor Relations Board

b. ANSI

c. United States Department of Labor

d. American Federation of Labor

12. A supervisor who works in a company that follows the parity principle of delegation would be most likely to say which of the following?

a. "I have adequate responsibility but not enough authority."

b. "I have adequate authority but not enough responsibility."

c. "I have an equal amount of authority and responsibility."

d. "I have adequate authority to meet my responsibility."

13. Your subordinate needs to learn a new task. What is the LEAST effective way for her to learn the new task?

a. Trial and error

b. Coaching

c. On-the-job training

d. Mentoring

14. You have recently been transferred, and you need to set performance standards for your new officers. You want to set the standards at a point that will elicit the best performance from them. To get your officers to perform at their best, how should you set the standards?

a. Set the standards very high and unreachable.

b. Set the standards high and reachable.

c. Set the standards low and easily reachable.

d. It doesn't matter where the standards are set; officers' performance is affected by other factors, not the set standards.

15. When assigning work, which of the following criteria would be best for a supervisor to use?

a. Allow the employees to select their task.

b. Assign all the easy work to slower employees.

c. Assign the harder tasks to the newer employees.

d. Assign tasks according to the ability of the employees.

16. You have been supervising a unit of 12 employees for just over a year. During that time, none of your employees have brought up any issues to you. It is probable that...

a. things are going just fine.

b. your employees are nervous about bringing issues to you.

c. due to the size of the unit, the employees already have their complaint structure set from within.

d. your employees are all self-starting and self-regulating.


17. Your supervisor informs you 20% of your employees have complained about your inconsistent evaluations and feedback. Your first action should be to...

a. admit that you have been and explain that your inconsistency was purposeful due to the weaknesses of these employees.

b. complain that these employees should have followed the chain of command and spoken with you.

c. ask for concrete examples of the inconsistencies so that the issue can be clear and you can address it.

d. offer to read up on management tactics and methods.

18. You've just learned you must ask your staff to work overtime this weekend. You should...

a. explain that they would be doing you a personal favor.

b. explain why it is necessary.

c. promise them time off in the future.

d. remind them that overtime is part of the job.

19. A formerly reliable worker has suddenly begun to arrive late to work more than twice a week. You should...

a. post a memo in the lounge and cc the memo to everybody in the unit spelling out the lateness policy.

b. discuss the matter privately with the employee and see if there is an underlying issue.

c. call an emergency staff meeting to get it out in the open

d. ask the employees friend to speak to him.

20. Which of the following terms is commonly used to refer to each employee's obligation to perform all duties to the best of his or her ability?

a. Authoritarian

b. Responsibility

c. Delegation

d. Accountability

21. To meet a deadline, a supervisor should…

a. schedule the work and monitor progress, and stay out of their way.

b. delegate all work.

c. bring in temp workers.

d. know the abilities and talents of her workers, make careful assignments, and monitor for progress. Pitch in when necessary.


22. While you were away for training, your supervisor assigned your employees to various tasks. Upon your return, you want to change the assignments to be more effective. You should…

a. discuss the change with your supervisor before implementing.

b. leave it alone and don't ask questions.

c. change it. No need to bother the boss.

d. stay late and do all the work yourself.

23. After reviewing an assignment completed by one of your employees, you realize changes need to be made. The employee objects to the changes. You should...

a. refer the employee to your supervisor.

b. ask the employee to read the proposed changes.

c. state that the decision is final. If they do not like it, they can seek employment elsewhere.

d. hear the employee out. Learn the reason for their objections, and then decide the best course of action.

24. What is the most important factor when preparing a holiday schedule for the unit?

a. Seniority.

b. Anticipated workload.

c. Preference of the employees.

d. How good the covering employees are.

25. For a new supervisor, which requires the most skill regarding inter-personal relations?

a. Challenging established norms.

b. Gaining the respect of older employees.

c. Training new hires.

d. Bringing up mistakes.

26. Which would be an indicator of high job satisfaction?

a. The team never works overtime.

b. The supervisor stays after hours for long-term planning.

c. The team gifts birthday and wedding gifts to each other.

d. The employees work hard to reach objectives, even if it means putting their personal agendas beneath that of the team.

27. When dealing with a complaint by an employee that is most likely unfounded, the complaint should be…

a. treated as founded until proven otherwise.

b. not important, as it is most likely nonsense.

c. an attempt by the employee at retribution against another.

d. seen as a psychotic episode of the employee.

28. You are attempting to teach a new hire how to use the work time recording system. The employee is having difficulty accessing the system, even though you find it a simple task. Before you spend more time working with the employee, you should...

a. review the steps you have already taught the employee to check for understanding.

b. admonish the employee for being so slow.

c. give the employee the manual and tell them to read it during lunch.

d. have the nearest employee try teaching it to the new employee.

29. An employee you supervise consistently complains when you assign a new task to him, even though he handles all work correctly and accurately. The complaints are beginning to irritate you and the other workers. You should...

a. give out the assignments privately.

b. threaten formal disciplinary charges.

c. explain the negative impact the complaints are having on the team.

d. ask one of the employees that is upset about the complaints to confront the employee.

30. Poor supervision has been blamed on the unwillingness of supervisors to manage their employees. The unwillingness to manage employees is based mainly on the supervisor's...

a. failure to embrace modern theories of supervision.

b. doubt about their ability to supervise.

c. fear of complaints from employees.

d. inability to demonstrate the same level of expertise as required of their employees.


31. Evaluation of employees is a major part of a supervisor's job. Which from the list below is a poor example of how to evaluate an employee?

a. Evaluations should be based on concrete examples of task performance.

b. Subjective judgment of vague outcomes should drive appraisals.

c. Evaluations should be based on objective criteria.

d. Evaluations should consider professional growth.

32. When is it least important to issue a written directive?

a. When the instructions are passed on from employee to employee.

b. When the instructions are very detailed.

c. When supervision will be present during the task.

d. When an employee has frequently failed to understand the instructions.

33. When accuracy and speed are important to a task, accuracy is considered more important because...

a. supervisors prefer accuracy.

b. accuracy drives a better reputation.

c. speed eventually fails.

d. correcting inaccurate work is very costly and labor intensive.

34. When an employee performs well, the supervisor should...

a. tell the employee they did well.

b. Call a meeting and ask for suggestions on improvement.

c. privately tell the employee "You're the best."

d. don't do anything. The employee will slack off.

35. You are a new supervisor. During your first few weeks, you put a stop to an unauthorized afternoon break where workers would go out for a beer. Several days later, a worker comes to you during the afternoon and asks if she can go to the pharmacy for some cold medicine. You should…

a. permit her to go.

b. ask her to sign out for the day and subtract it from her sick leave.

c. refuse.

d. tell her to take it during her meal time.


36. One of your workers is fast but inaccurate. Sometimes the mistakes take a long time to correct. A supervisor from another department wants to transfer him into her department and asks for an appraisal of the work quality. It is best to…

a. accentuate the positive.

b. allow the worker to start over.

c. give an honest assessment.

d. warn the new supervisor not to take the employee.

37. One of your employees fails to do their job. It is best practice to...

a. cool off and think it over.

b. give the employee another chance.

c. reprimand the employee and provide clear, concrete ways to improve.

d. ignore it.

38. One of your employees posts a poster that is offensive to the other employees and violates the sexual harassment policy of the organization. What should you do?

a. Have the offended employees complain to the offender.

b. Privately explain to the employee that the material is offensive and needs to come down.

c. Do nothing, freedom of speech.

d. Make a compromise.

39. A supervisor should...

a. follow the direction of the employees.

b. look to employees for assistance in making decisions.

c. always consult employees when making hard decisions.

d. always follow the advice of senior employees.

40. An employee has posted a sign above her desk that other employees have found offensive. You asked the employee to take it down, but she refuses stating "This is my space, and it is freedom of expression.". What should you do?

a. Wait until the issue has cooled down, then ask the employee to remove it as a favor.

b. Call the offended employees into a meeting with the offender and let them hash it out privately.

c. Check with company policy.

d. Calmly, but clearly instruct the employee to remove the sign, as it is creating a distractive environment and interfering with work.

41. How should a supervisor deal with an employee that lacks the self-confidence to get a task done, but is very capable of completing the task well?

a. Tell the employee to "suck it up."

b. Constantly praise the employee to boost confidence.

c. Inquire if the lack of self-confidence is due to relationship issues.

d. Compliment the employee's work when appropriate.

42. An employee was recently reprimanded for sleeping at work. During the disciplinary meeting, the employee reveals that he is having problems at home. What is an appropriate response by the supervisor?

a. Stay out of it.

b. Remove the reprimand from the employee record.

c. Offer to help at home.

d. Offer information about several support programs that might be helpful.

43. Your supervisor indicates that the transfer rate out of your department is very high. Which step would be helpful in beginning to address the problem?

a. Let the employees go home early that Friday.

b. Bring in coffee and donuts for the crew.

c. Discuss the issue with several employees to see if they can provide some insight as to the issue.

d. Consider those employees that left as quitters and don't look back.

44. Chain of command is defined as…

a. Every employee is under the direct control of one supervisor at any given time. There is a clear progression of supervision.

b. A way to control low-level employees.

c. A method for keeping employees happy.

d. A way to consolidate control of labor.

45. A new employee seems very capable but has been showing off computer skills to the irritation of the other employees. This employee is reliable and skilled; you would like him to fit in with the others. What should you do?

a. Nothing

b. Have two trusted employees talk to the new employee during lunch.

c. Commend the employee on is skill, but explain the situation.

d. Inform the senior employees that this is the way of the future, and they need to step up their computer game.

46. One of your employees comes to you and complains of sexual harassment by your supervisor. You should...

a. let the employee know you take her concerns seriously, then tell your supervisor what was said.

b. let the employee know you take her concerns seriously, then follow your agency Sexual harassment policy protocol.

c. act as a go-between to broker a compromise.

d. transfer the employee.

47. The worst reason for transferring an employee is to...

a. grant a request for a parent to work closer to the child's school.

b. avoid a harassment charge.

c. balance the workload between departments.

d. provide for greater training opportunities for the employee.

48. One way for a supervisor to earn the confidence of the employees is to...

a. sugar-coat bad news.

b. make quiet deals with employees.

c. tell the truth and follow through.

d. micro-manage.

49. A serious error was made in a project submitted by your unit. The best move would be to…

a. give a valid excuse.

b. identify the weak employee responsible.

c. Look for specific ways to correct the error and ensure it doesn't happen again.

d. punish those responsible.

50. Effective supervision means…

a. patience in supervising employees.

b. care in hiring workers.

c. meaningful evaluation.

d. fairness in discipline.

e. all of the above.

51. When assigning an employee to complete a monotonous task, it is important to have the employee…

a. perform the monotonous task first.

b. be on the lookout for mistakes and frequently check the work.

c. ask another employee to split the job.

d. perform this task late in the day, after lunch.

52. One of your employees committed a minor infraction of work rules. You should…

a. reprimand small things, so bug things don't occur.

b. sternly warn the employee.

c. speak to the employee and get an explanation for their behavior.

 d. inform your supervisor right away.

53. You have been issued orders to change working conditions that your employees disagree with. It is appropriate to tell your employees that…

a. you do not like the changes either, but you must follow them too.

b. that you will personally make it up the employees.

c. why the change is necessary and what benefit it will bring.

d. they do not have to follow the directive.

54. Your strongest employee complains to you that you give her more work than the other employees you should…

a. tell her she can handle it.

b. tell her that you ae recommending her for a promotion.

c. examine the workload and ensure the assignments are equitable.

d. tell her "to whom much is given, much is expected."

55. The number of employees a higher-level supervisor manages tends to be…

a. equal to that of lower level supervisors.

b. less than that of lower level supervisors.

c. more than that of lower level supervisors.

d. none of the above.

56. One managerial style assigns a set of tasks to a group of employees and then allows the group to decide how the tasks are broken up. One advantage of this management model is that it

a. increases job satisfaction.

b. always results in superior performance.

c. reduces the skill set each employee needs.

d. always results in faster completion.

57. You have discovered that you incorrectly reprimanded an employee for something they did not do. You should...

a. ignore the matter, the employee will eventually mess up and then you can give them a pass.

b. readily admit your mistake to the employee and take steps to prevent such a mistake in the future.

c. admit your mistake in an open letter to all of your employees

d. blame the mistake on the person who was the source of the misinformation.

58. You learn that one of your employees borrowed another employee's car and put a dent in it. The employee that damaged the car refuses to pay for the damage. The event occurred during the weekend and away from the worksite. What do you do?

a. Stay out of it.

b. Instruct the employee that damaged the car to pay for it.

c. Offer to pay for it.

d. Tell the employee with the damaged car to accept the loss and stay away from the other employee.

59. You have found out that an employee in your team has been stealing office supplies and selling them over the internet. What do you do?

a. Let it go. The supplies are not yours.

b. Report the theft to upper management and detail all factual information in a report.

c. Instruct the employee to return the supplies.

d. Lock up the supplies and inform the team the reason why.

60. A supervisor of a team of 25 employees spends most of her time reviewing the completed files of the employees. Analysis of this supervisor's work would suggest

a. the supervisor is doing a great job.

b. the supervisor needs to delegate the review responsibility to one or two experienced workers.

c. the supervisor needs to conduct training to ensure the accuracy of the files first time around.

d. the unit is functioning in an optimal way.

61. You have just been assigned to replace a supervisor known to demand employee compliance without question or feedback. You should...

a. continue with the strict discipline, as it is working.

b. begin by seeking feedback from employees as to the most effective way to perform their tasks.

c. discontinue all controls and allow workers to self-manage.

d. ask the employees what type of leadership they would best respond to.

62. When a new manager arrives in a department of twenty employees she observes that there is a tight-knit group of five employees who often volunteer to work together on projects. The group performs its tasks well, but the manager is threatened by the cohesiveness o this group. The manager should...

a. break the group up when assigning new tasks.

b. transfer one or more members.

c. leave the group as it is because it is functioning well.

d. leave the group as it is, but provide opportunities to include other workers in tasks with the group.

63. A middle manager is both a worker and a boss. When is it most appropriate to take on the role of the worker?

a. When the group isn't functioning well.

b. When the group has a conflict.

c. When the manager has the technical knowledge necessary for the project to proceed.

d. When there are many skilled employees in the unit.

64. A middle manager is both a worker and a boss. When is it most appropriate to take on the role of the boss?

a. When the group is functioning well on its own.

b. When the group has a conflict.

c. When the manager has the technical knowledge necessary for the project to proceed.

d. When there are many skilled employees in the unit.

65. A new supervisor was promoted from within the work-group. Before being promoted, he had an excellent record and was well respected by his co-workers. He has recently been assigned to a new employee that is having issues with the job. Specifically, the new worker is coming in late, making long personal phone calls, and the quality of their work is not on par with other new employees. The supervisor should...

a. send a memo to everybody on the unit spelling out the rules for lateness, phone calls, and work quality.

b. do nothing, as the employee will soon get up to speed.

c. ask two senior employees to speak with the new employee.

d. directly speak with the new employee. Ask what the issue is and instruct the new employee on work expectations.

66. A new supervisor was promoted from within the work-group. Prior to being promoted, he had an excellent record and was well respected by his co-workers. He has recently been assigned a new employee that is having issues with the job. Specifically, the new worker is having difficulty using a computer program necessary to complete certain aspects of the job. The supervisor should first...

a. send a memo to everybody on the unit spelling out how to use the program.

b. do nothing, as the employee will soon get up to speed.

c. ask two senior employees to coach with the new employee.

d. directly speak with the new employee. Find out what the issues are, and look for ways to help the new employee master the new program.

67. You are assigned to supervise a group of 25 employees. One of your employees comes to you and states he can no longer work for his direct supervisor. He states that he has tried to work out the issues with his supervisor, but has been ignored. You should…

a. tell the worker that they must work harder to get along.

b. transfer the employee.

c. dismiss the employee.

d. tell the employee that you will take their complaint seriously and will discuss the matter directly with their supervisor.

68. Which statement is most accurate?

a. Behavior is a better indicator for success than personality.

b. Most times it is best to wait before acting, as most times a problem with go away on its own.

c. Poor work habits are harder to break than poor performance.

d. When thinking about an employee's behavior, it is most important to consider the motives behind the behavior.

69. You have been a supervisor of a work group for six months. One of your employees has consistently underperformed and has made numerous costly mistakes. You have directly spoken with this employee, provided additional training, and have written detailed letters of reprimand. There has been no change in performance or behavior. You have been told by other employees that this worker has always performed this way, but that previous supervisors have ignored it or have transferred the employee. You should...

a. ignore it too.

b. ask the employee to resign.

c. transfer the employee.

d. discuss the issue with your supervisor and suggest exploring termination proceedings.

70. One of the employees you supervise is very assertive and effective. The employee is polite, but clearly does not feel the other employees in the unit contribute much to the success of the unit. The other employees are resentful and feel they are constantly being outdone by the high quality of the employee's work. They have come to you for assistance. You should...

a. Acknowledge the high quality of the work, but stress that the ability to get along with the team is as important as good work.

b. Tell the complaining employees that they need to step up their game.

c. Tell the high performing employee to tone it down and work slower.

d. Transfer the employee to a better unit

71. As a supervisor, you have to make an important decision and would like input. You should...

a. consult with everybody in your unit.

b. talk only with another supervisor from a different department.

c. talk with a retired employee who still keeps tabs on the group.

d. discuss the matter with your supervisor and a few trusted employees from your group.

72. Which statement is least accurate?

a. Most workers want to satisfy physical, social, and emotional needs.

b. A supervisor can influence the personal lives of the workers they supervise.

c. Supervisors who spend time learning about their employees are wasting valuable time.

d. Most workers want responsibilities they can handle, success they can demonstrate, and recognition for work well done.

73. You are the manager of a team of 25 employees and 5 supervisors. One of your employees complains to you that his supervisor is not doing his job. He complains that there is no meaningful feedback and that the supervisor often assigns his own work to subordinate employees. The employee states that when he has raised concerns to the supervisor directly, he has been blown off and given additional work to do. What should you do?

a. Transfer the employee, so they will be happier.

b. Admonish the employee for not following the chain of command.

c. Tell the employee that you take the complaint seriously and then investigate the matter thoroughly.

d. Send a memo to all the supervisors instructing them to provide better feedback and complete their work themselves.

74. A supervisor finds she rates two of her ten employees very highly because they have similar backgrounds to her own. The supervisor should…

a. look for ways to be as subjective as possible when evaluating employees.

b. look for ways to be as objective as possible when evaluating employees.

c. evaluate all employees equally, regardless of performance.

d. lower the rating of the two employees she identifies with.

75. You supervise an employee who is a perfectionist and suffers anxiety when a project isn't perfect. He is showing signs of "burnout". What should you do?

a. Sign up the employee for staff development in assertiveness.

b. Sign up the employee for staff development in goal-setting.

c. Discuss with the employee the results of working too hard and suggest an assessmentthat evaluates how exact the next project has to be. Discuss the standards for the upcoming project and include how it need not be perfect.

d. Leave the employee alone. Hard workers should be encouraged to keep up the good work.

76. Which of these statements is least accurate?

a. It doesn't matter if a team thinks the agency's climate is fair and positive.

b. Teams are likely to have informal authority and structure.

c. Supervisors should accept subgroups that form within a team.

d. It is not acceptable for a supervisor to be viewed as an outsider that enforces rules on the team with no input from the team.

77. When conducting a disciplinary meeting, the supervisor should do all the following except:

a. State the purpose of the interview.

b. State the problem and review expectations.

c. Be specific.

d. Promise the employee to keep it within the team.

78. You have just been promoted from a worker role into the role of supervisor on a different team. You are assigned to replace an employee from this new team that had held the supervisor role on a provisional basis. The former supervisor is now very bitter and is subtly undermining your authority. What should you do?

a. Transfer the employee.

b. Put a disciplinary letter in the employee's file.

c. Speak with your supervisor concerning the problem.

d. Speak with the employee directly about the problem.


79. Which statement is correct?

a. Informal work organizations are beyond the control of supervision.

b. Informal work organizations can be very powerful.

c. Informal work organizations seldom carry any power.

d. Informal work organizations only result in socializing.

80. You supervise a team of 30 employees. One of your responsibilities includes assigning overtime. Most employees are OK to deal with concerning the overtime, and you are careful to assign it equitably. One employee has accused you of assigning him to work overtime on the days before holidays. How should you respond?

a. Only assign the employee to work the night before holidays in the future.

b. Never assign the employee to work the night before holidays in the future.

c. Re-examine your assignments to confirm you are fair, then discuss this with the employee.

d. Do nothing.

81. When supervising, it's best to...

a. focus on appearances.

b. refine hidden expectations.

c. focus on employees' attitude toward the job as basis for evaluation.

d. know the standards and ensure the employees know them as well,

82. You manage a team of 25 employees and 5 supervisors. One of your employees complains to you about her immediate supervisor. She states that the supervisor is constantly interrupting her team during work to talk about her projects. The employee states that because so much of their time is taken up by their supervisor, it is harder to complete the workload. You should…

a. transfer this employee.

b. ignore the employee's complaint.

c. demote the supervisor.

d. discuss the issue directly with the supervisor and come up with a plan to support the supervisor with her projects.

83. Which is an appropriate statement for a supervisor to make to an employee?

a. "I'm concerned that you are taking too many cigarette breaks, and that it is affecting your work performance. Please limit your breaks to the assigned times."

b. "You want to go to a conference next week? No chance, buddy!"

c. "You must have a weak bladder if you need so many coffee breaks."

d. "That skirt looks hot!"

84. New supervisors can expect to face all of the following except...

a. difficulty making decisions for fear of failure.

b. spending too much time procrastinating and over planning.

c. instant success and flawless transitions.

d. challenges integrating into the team.


85. Which of the following is not true about planning and organizing work?

a. Good planning skills are not as important as good communication skills.

b. Well-written training manuals allow a supervisor to manage by exception

c. Every operation needs planning, even when it looks routine

d. A good supervisor should have contingency and backup plans for operating during a crisis.

86. You gave a clear directive to an employee to perform a task. When the task is not completed, you approach the employee about his failure, and he responds that he thought it was optional. What should you do?

a. Nothing; move on.

b. Reprimand the employee.

c. Continue the conversation to find out if the failure to complete the task was an honest misunderstanding or a willful refusal.

d. Assign the task to someone else.


87. You have recently been appointed to supervise a team of 25 employees and 5 supervisors. You immediately realize that there is a strong "pecking order" between the newer and more senior workers. The newer employees are not allowed to complete certain tasks even though the task is in their job description. Newer employees have expressed that they are eager to learn these tasks.

What should you do?

a. Leave the structure in place.

b. Send out a memo demanding that it stop.

c. Slowly, but firmly begin changing policies.

d. Choose one senior employee to an example of.

87. You supervise an employee who is enthusiastic, hardworking, fast, and reliable. He is always clean but often appears sloppy in appearance. What should you do?

a. Nothing, if it doesn't interfere with work.

b. Send out a memo on personal appearance.

c. Have two trusted employees address the issue.

d. Call the employee's wife.

88. Two employees you supervise appear to be developing a romantic relationship. You should...

a. Do nothing, as long as it doesn't interfere with work.

b. Tell the employees to 'cease and desist'.

c. Transfer one employee.

d. Begin termination proceedings.

89. You supervise a team of 25 employees and 5 supervisors. Two of your employees are married. You want to promote the wife into a supervisory role. What should you do?

a. Don't promote the worker, as it will be a conflict of interest.

b. Transfer the employee to a different team than the spouse will be supervising to avoid conflict of interest.

c. Promote the worker and don't worry about it.

d. Request the employee resign.

90. You supervise a unit of 25 employees and five supervisors. A vacancy for a supervisory job has opened and you are considering hiring Jane for the job. Just as you are preparing to submit the paperwork appointing her to the supervisor position, she informs you that she has been offered a similar supervisor position with a competing agency. You should...

a. let her go because she obviously wasn't happy with your team anyway.

b. tell her that you would like to keep her as an employee and offer her the supervisor job.

c. call the new company up and explain that she lacks loyalty.

d. terminate her, so the other employees will remain in their place.

91. All the following is true except...

a. support from supervisors can be stressful to an employee.

b. an employee's sense of self-esteem is an excellent way to evaluate performance.

c. supervisory behavior has a great effect on employee performance.

d. employees who are part of the decision-making process can have more satisfaction at work.

# Answers to practice questions:

1. The correct answer is (c). Tell the employee to call the training office and see if the application was lost. At this point, it is prudent to follow up. Having the employee make the call herself is a good way to foster independence and self-reliance. It would not be necessary to step in yet.

2. The correct answer is (c). Upper management typically decides what planning is done by lower level supervisors and employees.

3. The correct answer is (a.) The Occupational Safety and Health Administration (OSHA) is chartered to set safety standards, investigate work-related accidents, and enforce worker safety laws.

4. The correct answer is (d). The term "line employee" is synonymous with "front-line employee." Line employees are those most directly in charge of the meeting of company goals and objectives.

5. The correct answer is (a). Marital problems are usually dealt with outside of the workplace. In as much as marital problems may affect job performance, they are not job-related.

6. The correct answer is (c). Marital status is clearly an unacceptable question. Consult the "Interview Question" guide included earlier in this book for more insight as to inappropriate/ appropriate questions.

7. The correct answer is (c). Maslow was famous for developing his hierarchy of needs. Most basic needs are on the bottom and self-actualization appears at the top. For an employee to become self-actualize and perform at their best, the other basic needs must be met first.

8. The correct answer is (b). Departmental discipline is the responsibility of the department supervisor. The shop steward is a union position. The president deals with larger company-wide issues, and the human relations manager interacts with the public.

9. The correct answer is (b ). Out of all of these choices, "developing employee benefits" is a task that lies outside of employee production and performance. The controlling process deals directly with production and performance.

10. The correct answer is (a). The National Labor Relations board is authorized to enforce labor laws such as overtime, minimum wage, etc.

11. The correct answer is (d). The American Federation of Labor is one of the nation's largest and oldest labor unions.

12. The correct answer is (d). According to the Parity Principle of delegation, the manager should keep a balance between authority and responsibility. According to this principle, if an employee is given a responsibility to perform a task, then at the same time he or she should be given enough independence and power to carry out that task effectively.

13. The correct answer is (a). Learning a new task through trial and error is not only time consuming, learning be demoralizing for the subordinate if the task is not learned quickly. It could also lead to mistakes that may need to be corrected by others.

14. The correct answer is (b) By setting the standards high, but reachable you will create a realistic expectation to perform at a high level and will show your subordinates that you understand the situation in a realistic way.

15. The correct answer is (d). Assign tasks according to the ability of the employees. For the unit to function, the supervisor must be aware of each employee's abilities. By assigning tasks by employee ability, there is a high probability that the task can be completed correctly.

16. The correct answer is (b). Your employees are nervous about bringing issues to you. As a new supervisor, your employees may not know how you will react when confronted with an issue. It is most important here to begin to open up appropriate lines of communication so that your employees will trust you enough to raise issues.

17. The correct answer is (c). Ask for concrete examples of the inconsistencies so that the issue can be clear and you can address it. In this way, you can identify the problem and correct it. It is always hurtful to hear negative feedback in this fashion, but you must resist the temptation to blame others or seek retribution.

18. The correct answer is (b). Explain why it is necessary. Assigning overtime may be an unpleasant task. Explaining the reason and benefit of the overtime to the employees may help them understand the benefit this over time will have on the mission of the team.

19. The correct answer is (b). Discuss the matter privately with the employee and see if there is an underlying issue. There may be an underlying and correctable issue that can be resolved easily. Since the employee was once reliable, it should be a goal to return the employee back to the status of "reliable" once again.

20. B Employees have the responsibility to follow orders from their supervisors. The other choices are all skills and tasks supervisors employ.

21. The correct answer is (d). Know the abilities and talents of her workers, make careful assignments, and monitor for progress. Pitch in when necessary. In this way, the supervisor can effectively delegate and ensure high-quality results. If possible, the supervisor could also assist in areas requiring expertise to make the project progress efficiently.

22. The correct answer is (a). Discuss the change with your supervisor before implementing. Keep the chain of command in mind here. Your supervisor's directive stands until rescinded. You must first get permission to change the directive.

23. The correct answer is (d). Hear the employee out. Learn the reason for their objections, and then decide the best course of action. Don't be too fast to dismiss the objections of an employee. There may be real insight and benefit to what they have to say. If you still don't agree, then you can move towards disciplinary proceedings, but that shouldn't be your first move.

24. The correct answer is (b). Anticipated workload. The mission and the needs of the agency must come first above the vacation desires of the employees.

25. The correct answer is (a). Challenging established norms. Established norms may be deeply ingrained into the culture of the agency. Changing how employees do things may be met with real resistance.

26. The correct answer is (d). The employees work hard to reach objectives, even if it means putting their personal agendas beneath that of the team. When there is high worker morale, the employees are more willing to remain focused and work hard to reach objectives.

27. The correct answer is (a). Treated as founded until proven otherwise. Even if a complaint is most likely unfounded, there is still a chance it is founded. Once the complaint is proven unfounded, then the employee can be counseled about making an unfounded complaint.

28. The correct answer is (a). Review the steps you have already taught the employee to check for understanding. In this fashion, you can confirm that the employee understands what you have previously taught so that you can now move forward.

29. The correct answer is (c). Explain the negative impact the complaints are having on the team. The employee may not be aware of the impact their complaints are having. Clearly and specifically explain how the negativity is damaging to the team.

30. The correct answer is (b). Doubt about their ability to supervise. Most supervisors who fail to take action do so because they are insecure about their own ability as managers.

31. The correct answer is (b). Subjective judgment of vague outcomes should drive appraisals. Subjective assessments are based on feelings and emotions, not evidence and facts. If challenged, subjective assessments are hard to defend because there is little factual evidence for the assessment.

32. The correct answer is (c). When supervision will be present during the task. When supervision is located close to the work site, there is less of a need for a written directive because the supervision can readily step in and direct operations.

33. The correct answer is (d). Correcting inaccurate work is very costly and labor intensive. The old adage "Haste makes Waste" makes sense here. Rushing through things can be more expensive than deliberate, thoughtful work.

34. The correct answer is (a). Tell the employee they did well. Use specific descriptions of the work they did so you can reinforce how to complete work well in the future.

35. The correct answer is (a). Permit her to go. The reason is that they are two separate issues. This worker asked for permission instead just going on her own.

36. The correct answer is (c). Give an honest assessment. Honesty, though initially painful, may lead to mutual respect and a better understanding of the issues.

37. The correct answer is (c). Reprimand the employee and provide clear, concrete ways to improve. It is very important to provide this feedback as soon as possible after an incident. The idea is that the issue will still be fresh in the worker's mind.

38. The correct answer is (b). Privately explain to the employee that the material is offensive and needs to come down. Allowing offensive material to remain in the workplace is unacceptable and could lead to larger problems.

39. The correct answer is (b). Look to employees for assistance in making decisions. While it is fine to consult with employees to gain insight, ultimately, it is the supervisor who must make hard decisions.

40. The correct answer is (d). Calmly, but clearly instruct the employee to remove the sign, as it is creating a distractive environment and interfering with work. In this case, the behavior has become insubordinate. If the matter persisted, and you were sure the employee understands the implications for their behavior, you should begin formal disciplinary proceedings.

41. The correct answer is (d). Compliment the employees work when appropriate. Overly praising an employee is just as bad as not praising them. When commenting an employee's work, be specific so that you further guide the employee towards more success.

42. The correct answer is (d). Offer information about several support programs that might be helpful. You do not want to ignore the substandard behavior, nor do you want to diagnose the employee's problem. Making a referral is a safe suggestion that may help.

43. The correct answer is (c). Discuss the issue with several employees to see if they can provide some insight as to the issue. In this case, you want to find some insight into the issue of employees transferring out. Talking with several employees may provide useful information.

44. (a). Every employee is under the direct control of one supervisor at any given time. Under the chain of command, an employee knows who is in charge. Generally, higher ranking leaders do not directly interfere with employees more than one level below them.

45. The correct answer is (c). Commend the employee on is skill, but explain the situation. Open dialog here would be useful. You do not want to stifle the new employee, but you want him or her to fit in.

46. (b). Let the employee know you take her concerns seriously, then follow your agency Sexual harassment policy protocol. Following a protocol is the correct way to see that the issue is correctly dealt with. If there is no protocol, you would be expected to bring the matter above your supervisor's head to the next level of management.

47. The correct answer is (b). Avoid a harassment charge. Issues of harassment should be dealt with directly and according to the protocol set up by the agency. Transferring an employee is only a temporary fix and further weakens the agency.

48. The correct answer is (c). Tell the truth and follow through. Honesty is one of the hallmarks of a great leader.

49. The correct answer is (c). Look for specific ways to correct the error and ensure it doesn't happen again. Serious mistakes weaken an agency, yet you cannot go back in time. The best option here is to design policies and methods to prevent such mistakes in the future.

50. The correct answer is (e). All of the above. Patience in supervising employees, care in hiring workers, meaningful evaluation, and fairness in discipline are all elements of effective supervision.

51. The best answer is (b). Be on the lookout for mistakes and frequently check the work. Mistakes are frequently very expensive and are more common with monotonous tasks. It is best to check work at frequent intervals to prevent mistakes in repetition.

52. The correct answer is (c). Speak to the employee and get an explanation for their behavior. It is best not to immediately jump to conclusions. Find out the reasons first, and then act.

53. The correct answer is (c). Explain why the change is necessary and what benefit it will bring. Sometimes a change has a very valid reason, and employees may be more receptive to it if they understand how it will help.

54. The correct answer is (c). Examine the workload and ensure the assignments are equitable. It may be possible you give this worker more to do because of the quality of her work. Respect her complaint and take it seriously.

55. The correct answer is (b). Less than that of lower level supervisors. In most organizations, the lower level supervisors directly supervise many employees.

56. The correct answer is (a). Increases job satisfaction. Often times the members of a team know best how to deploy their resources and feel satisfaction in doing so.

57. The correct answer is (b). Readily admit your mistake to the employee and take steps to prevent such a mistake in the future. You cannot change the past, but you can take steps to prevent these mistakes in the future. Taking responsibility for your actions will increase trust between you and your employees.

58. The correct answer is (a). Stay out of it. This matter occurred away from work. If it does not interfere with work, it is best to stay out of it.

59. The correct answer is (b). Report the theft to upper management and detail all factual information in a report. Theft is a major problem and cannot be looked over. Employees who steal will most likely keep stealing.

60. The correct answer is (b). The supervisor needs to delegate the review responsibility to one or two experienced workers. The time spent reviewing completed work would be much better spent supervising.

61. The correct answer is (b). Begin by seeking feedback from employees as to the most effective way to perform their tasks. You don't want to dramatically change things, nor do you want to ignore the issue by leaving things along. Start by talking to your employees, and then develop a plan to move forward.

62. The correct answer is (d). Leave the group as it is, but provide opportunities to include other workers in tasks with the group. Informal work groups can be a real asset and raise productivity. They can also form a clique. It would be wise to keep the group together but also provide for opportunities to interact with others.

63. The correct answer is (c). When the manager has technical knowledge necessary for the project to proceed. This is the best use of the manager's time. The manager should resist the temptation to spend too much of their time doing the work and should instead focus on supporting the staff in their mission.

64. The correct answer is (b). When the group has a conflict. In times of conflict within the team, it is the responsibility of the boss to step in and help resolve it.

65. The correct answer is (d). Directly speak with the new employee. Ask what the issue is and instruct the new employee on work expectations. Direct conversation is a clear way to understand what the issues are and direct the employee to behave in an appropriate manner.

66. The correct answer is (d). Directly speak with the new employee. Find out what the issues are, and look for ways to help the new employee master the new program. Direct communication here is the key to success. It will allow you to assess where the issue lies.

67. The correct answer is (d). Tell the employee that you will take their complaint seriously and will discuss the matter directly with their supervisor. The reassurance of taking the complaint seriously will go a long way to working to resolve the issue. Following through by talking to the supervisor may help to bring to light additional issues. Once you have collected enough information, an informed plan or decision can be made.

68. Which statement is most accurate? (a). Behavior is a better indicator for success than personality. Behaviors can be measured and used as evidence for making informed decisions.

69. The correct answer is (d). Discuss the issue with your supervisor and suggest exploring termination proceedings. Though termination is a very serious action, there is substantial evidence and data to support it at this time. Careful documentation and objective evaluation will be necessary to make a case for termination.

70. The correct answer is (a). Acknowledge the high quality of the work, but stress that the ability to get along with the team is as important as good work. You do not want to stifle the excellent work of this employee, but you want him or her to become a part of the team. Communicating this should be effective.

71. The correct answer is (d). Discuss the matter with your supervisor and a few trusted employees from your group. This will give you valuable feedback from different, yet trusted points of view.

72. The correct answer is (d). Most workers want responsibilities they can handle, success they can demonstrate, and recognition for work well done. Employees find greater job satisfaction in this way and perform better.

73. The correct answer is (c). It is important to take the complaint seriously and investigate. If the complaint is founded, you have the opportunity to speak with the supervisor and address the issue.

74. The correct answer is (b). Look for ways to be as objective as possible when evaluating employees. This insight is an opportunity for this supervisor to work toward more objective observations which may increase the satisfaction all of the employees feel.

75. The correct answer is (c). Discuss with the employee the results of working too hard and suggest an assessment to evaluate how exact the next project has to be. Discuss the standards for the upcoming project and include how it need not be perfect. By addressing these issues, the employee may find a better level of comfort in completing tasks and projects.

76. The correct answer is (a). It doesn't matter if a team thinks the agency's climate is fair and positive. It is very important that the team thinks the agency's climate is fair and positive. If the employees lose faith in this, their job satisfaction and quality will suffer.

77. The correct answer is (d). Promise the employee to keep it within the team. The reason for not making this promise is that you have no idea of the outcome of this meeting. Matters may come to light that necessitate the issue going above the team.

78. The correct answer is (c). Speak with your supervisor concerning the problem. This is one of the few times you should go to your supervisor with a problem concerning one of your employees.

79. The correct answer is (b). Informal work organizations can be very powerful. Informal work groups can help determine the climate and job satisfaction of the group.

80. The correct answer is (c). Re-examine your assignments to confirm you are fair, then discuss this with the employee. This is an effective way to deal with this issue. First, it is always possible you made a mistake. If you find no mistake, you can present objective facts from your findings to the employee.

81. The correct answer is (d). Know the standards and ensure the employees know them as well. Having clear standards is one way to communicate expectations to the employees.

82. The correct answer is (d). Discuss the issue directly with the supervisor and come up with a plan to support the supervisor with her projects.

83. The correct answer is (a). "I'm concerned that you are taking too many cigarette breaks, and that it is affecting your work performance. Please limit your breaks to the assigned times." This statement clearly identifies the problem and instructs the employee what the appropriate behavior is.

84. The correct answer is (c). Instant success and flawless transitions. This is seldom the case. Learning how to supervise takes time.

85. The correct answer is (a). Good planning skills are not as important as good communication skills. Both of these are essential

86. The correct answer is (c). Continue the conversation to find out if the failure to complete the task was an honest misunderstanding or a willful refusal.

87. The correct answer is (c). Slowly, but firmly begin changing policies. It takes time to change agency culture. If you make a commitment to the change and are consistent in your efforts, the culture will change.

87. The correct answer is (a). Nothing, as long as it doesn't interfere with work. The one exception to this would be if the employee needs to interact with the public, as a sloppy appearance would reflect poorly on the agency.

88. The correct answer is (a). Do nothing, as long as it doesn't interfere with work. This is the case when neither employee is responsible for supervising the other. If one is a supervisor, a transfer might be appropriate.

89. The correct answer is (b). Transfer the employee to a different team than the spouse will be supervising to avoid conflict of interest. The transfer would be appropriate in this case.

90. The correct answer is (b). Tell her that you would like to keep her as an employee and offer her the supervisor job. You should do your best to keep this valuable employee.

91. The correct answer is (b). An employee's sense of self-esteem is an excellent way to evaluate performance

# Glossary

**Abraham Maslow** Humanistic psychologist known for his "Hierarchy of Needs" and the concept of "self-actualization"

**Action Learning** Training in which teams get an actual problem, work on solving it and commit to an action plan, and are accountable for carrying it out

**Authority** the power to hold people accountable for their actions and to make decisions concerning the use of organizational resources

**Avoiding** a conflict resolution style by which one party wants to remain neutral, stay away from conflict, or postpone the conflict to gather information or let things cool down

**Blocking Roles** prevent the group from functioning effectively because they attack other group members or divert the group's attention

**Budget** a summary of intended expenditures along with proposals for how to meet them

**Command Groups** Groups that are determined by the organization chart and composed of individuals who report directly to a given manager.

**Compromising** Managing conflict by giving up part of what you want, to provide at least some satisfaction for both parties

**Conceptual Skill** The cognitive ability to see the organization as a whole and the relationships among its parts

**Confronting** normal reaction when conflict occurs: tendency to approach or engage in conflict; one actively discusses issues and engages in conflict situations; when disagreements occur the confronter wants to get all issues on the table ASAP (part of competition, compromise, collaboration, accommodation)

**Controlling** a management function that involves establishing clear standards to determine whether or not an organization is progressing toward its goals and objectives, rewarding people for doing a good job, and taking corrective action if they are not

**Decision Making** Understanding information and reaching a conclusion to solve problems.

**Derven** He suggested that the (appraisal) process is so inherently flawed that it may be impossible to perfect it

**Diagnostic Skill** Is used to investigate problems, decide on a remedy, and implement a solution.

**Douglas McGregor** Theory X and Theory Y. 'Theory X', which stresses the importance of strict supervision and external rewards and penalties; and 'Theory Y', which highlights the motivating role of job satisfaction and allows scope for workers to approach tasks creatively.

**Financial Budget** Sources and uses for cash

**First Line Managers** Managers who supervise operatives (also known as supervisors).

**Forcing Managing** conflict by satisfying your own needs or advancing your own ideas, with no concern for the needs or ideas of the other and no concern for the harm done to the relationship.

**Frederick Herzberg** Created Theory of Motivation-Hygiene/Two Factor Theory of Job Satisfaction: Noted that there is a difference between just being satisfied and being motivated

**Frederick Taylor** Father of scientific management also known as Taylorism. He created a theory a theory of management that analyzes and synthesizes workflows. Its main objective is improving economic efficiency, especially labor productivity. It was one of the earliest attempts to apply science to the engineering of processes and to management.

**Friendship Groups** An informal group composed of employees who enjoy one another's company and socialize with one another.

**Functional Groups** Created by the organization to accomplish specific goals within an unspecified time frame

**Global Environment** The set of global forces and conditions that operate beyond an organization's boundaries but affect a manager's ability to acquire and utilize resources

**Group Norms** General expectations of a demand nature regarding acceptable group behavior

**Group Structure** stable pattern of relationships that maintain the group and help it achieve goal, roles, and norms

**Hierarchy of Needs Maslow's pyramid of human needs.** At the bottom are the most important things: life, food and physiological needs. At the top are psychological needs. One has to satisfy physiological needs first like eating and drinking, and then worry about safety, shelter, and eventually psychological needs.

**Henry Mintzberg** Divided manager's job into three types: interpersonal, informational, decisional

**Informer Role** Role of finding facts and giving advice or opinions in an organization

**Interest Groups** Groups of people who work together for similar interests or goals.

**Interpersonal Skill** Involves human relations, or the manager's ability to interact effectively with organizational members.

**Job Analysis** a purposeful, systematic process for collecting information on the important work-related aspects of a job

**Kurt Lewin** Father of modern social psychology. behavior is a function of both the person and the environment

**Lawrie** Sees appraisal as the most crucial aspect of organizational life.

**Leadership** The ability to influence individuals or groups to achieve organizational goals

**Leading management** process of guiding and motivating employees to meet an organization's objectives

**Maintenance Roles** patterns of behavior that help the group develop and maintain good member relationships, group cohesiveness and effective levels of conflict

**Management** the process used to accomplish organizational goals through planning, organizing, leading, and controlling people and other organizational resources

**Middle Level Managers** Managers who are neither executives nor first-level supervisors, but who serve as a link between the two groups.

**Modern Appraisal** a future-oriented approach and is developmental in nature; recognizes employees as individuals and focuses on their development

**Nonmonetary budget** planned operations in non-financial terms

**Operating budget** planned operations in financial terms

**Organizational Development** plan describes how the company will organize the work that needs to be accomplished. Kurt Lewin is father of this.

**Organizational Structure** the arrangement of jobs and the relationships among the jobs in an organization.

**Organization Charts** Show the hierarchical structure and relationships within an organization.

**Organizing** Management process of determining how best to arrange an organization's resources and activities into a coherent structure

**Outsourcing** A decision by a corporation to turn over much of the responsibility for production to independent suppliers.

**Performance Appraisal** an evaluation that measures employee performance against established standards in order to make decisions about promotions, compensation, training, or termination

**Personnel Recruitment** The process of determining staffing needs, predicting turnover and vacancies, and identifying and recruiting potential replacements to maintain the staffing levels required to meet program objectives

**Peter Drucker** A management theorist who is credited with introducing the idea of management by objectives (MBO). This groups the role of management into five different operations including the setting of objectives for the organization, the organization of the work, the motivation of employees, the measurement of the job being done and the development of people.

**Peter Senge** Calls for five disciplines in the learning organization:

◦System Thinking

◦Personal Mastery

◦Mental Models

◦Shared Vision

◦Team Learning

**Planning** The process of anticipating future events and determining strategies to achieve organizational objectives in the future

**Political Skill** The ability to understand others at work and to use that knowledge to influence others to act in ways that enhance one's personal or organizational objectives.

**Problem Solving** thinking and behavior directed toward attaining a goal that is not readily available

**Renumeration** Payment for work done

**Robert Blake and Jane Mouton** Created a management model that conceptualizes management styles and relations. Their Grid uses two axis. "Concern for people" is plotted using the vertical axis and "Concern for task" is along the horizontal axis.

**Role Ambiguity** Uncertainty about what the organization expects from the employee in terms of what to do or how to do it

**Smoothing** Minimizing differences and emphasizing common interests; unassertive and cooperative

**Sociotechnical Systems Theory A** Theory that examines both social and technical characteristics of tasks and how work is organized, focusing on the interaction between people and technologies

**Summative Evaluation** An evaluation of training program conducted after program has been implemented in order to assess outcomes

**Task Groups** also called secondary groups; groups formed for the purpose of completing tasks, such as solving problems or making decisions

**Taylorism** Implemented by Fredrick W. Taylor, scientific management to reduce waste, was resented by many although he brought concrete improvements of productivity

**Technical Skill** the expertise necessary to be proficient with methods and processes to run front-line operations

**Union** an organization of employees formed to bargain with the employer

**Work Roles** The activities performed by one or more group members that help the group accomplish its task and pursue its goals

Made in the USA
Las Vegas, NV
07 September 2023

77172216R00056